40.–

Leasing in Germany

Leasing in Germany

Legal, Accounting and Taxation Issues

Published by:
Arthur Andersen & Co. GmbH
Wirtschaftsprüfungsgesellschaft
Steuerberatungsgesellschaft

VERLAG NEUE WIRTSCHAFTS-BRIEFE
HERNE / BERLIN

Die Deutsche Bibliothek — CIP-Einheitsaufnahme

Leasing in Germany: legal, accounting, and taxation issues / publ. by: Arthur Andersen & Co. GmbH, Wirtschaftsprüfungsgesellschaft, Steuerberatungsgesellschaft. — Herne; Berlin: Verl. Neue Wirtschafts-Briefe, 1991

ISBN 3-482-45221-0

NE: Arthur Andersen und Co. <Frankfurt, Main>

ISBN 3-482-**45221**-0

Druck: H. Rademann GmbH, 4710 Lüdinghausen

PREFACE

The brochure „Leasing in Germany“ intends to provide a concise overview of the German leasing market, its important features in relation to the use of leasing as a principal financing technique and its position in international leasing structures.

The brochure was prepared by the Financial Services Group of Arthur Andersen & Co. GmbH, Frankfurt am Main, and published by Arthur Andersen & Co. GmbH.

The booklet was written by Wolfgang Oho and Klaus Weinand-Härer. Legal features were covered by Dr. Eberhard Kalbfleisch. The section on tax incentives for leasing in West-Berlin was contributed by Walter Rieckmann.

Many people have assisted greatly in the preparation of this booklet. We thank each of the contributors for devoting their time in revising, up-dating and writing the material for this publication.

We have very much appreciated the support of Rosheen Quraishi for help in the English language and proof reading. Finally, our thanks go to Sabine Jendges for her valued assistance in preparing the script.

To the best of our knowledge and belief, the information provided in this brochure is correct at the time of going to press. However, it is intented to be a general guide and we recommend that professional advice is sought before action is taken on any specific issues.

Frankfurt am Main, December 1990

CONTENTS

PAGE

PAGE

CONTENTS OF THE APPENDICES

1. INTRODUCTION

Leasing was initially introduced to Germany with the establishment of the first leasing companies in 1962. Since then the leasing market has grown rapidly, with more than 1,000 leasing companies having been established by 1988. After a period of consolidation in 1984, leasing investments are now growing faster than total economic investment as a whole, and the West German market is now the most developed in Europe (see appendix I).

A tendency to use leasing as a new marketing instrument can also be identified. In comparison to the U.S.A. (29 %), in Germany leasing made up only 10 % of total investments during 1988. Based on the developments of recent years a significant increase in German leasing investment can be anticipated for the future.

An increasing number of leveraged and cross-border leasing transactions now make use of the varying treatments of leasing contracts under tax considerations and different jurisdictions. As a preparation for the internal European Market 1992 a large number of leasing companies have built up international connections, or established foreign subsidiaries or cooperation agreements in anticipation of the increasing requirements of the marketplace.

2. TYPES OF LEASING CONTRACTS

In Germany a general distinction is made between leases of real estate and of movable property, and between finance, operating and special leases. This distinction is illustrated in the following sections.

2.1. Finance leases

Finance (or financial) leases are characterised by a fixed initial lease term, within which neither the lessee nor the lessor can terminate the lease contract. In many cases certain options are granted at the end of this initial lease period. Depending on who obtains economic ownership of the leased asset, it is capitalised in the financial statements of either the lessor or of the lessee (see section 4). The finance lease is usually used mostly for long-term contracts on movable property or real estate.

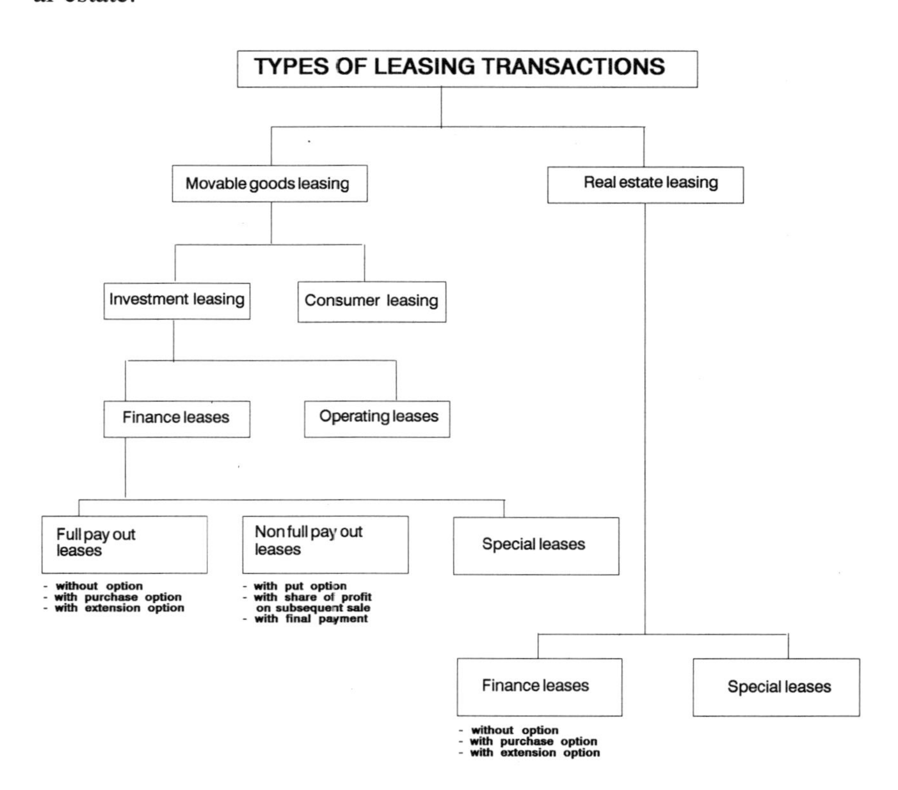

A further distinction must be made between full pay out and non-full pay out finance leases, which are treated differently for German tax and accounting purposes. Both types of leases have a fixed initial lease term, within which the contract cannot be terminated by either party. Under a full pay out lease the lease payments during the initial lease term are equal to at least the lessor's total cost, including depreciation, financing costs and administration fees. Under a non full pay out lease the lease payments during the initial lease term do not cover the lessor's costs; the residual value remaining at the end of the initial lease term must be covered either by means of the exercise of a put option by the lessor or by means of the sale of the asset at its fair market value.

2.2. Operating leases

There are no fixed initial lease terms for operating lease contracts, i.e. either party can at any time terminate the lease contract at short notice. The operating lease can therefore be compared to the renting of an asset to another person or company.

In relation to the useful life of the asset, operating leases are usually short-term contracts. The lessor must lease the asset several times in order to recover his costs and will therefore continue to bear a certain element of commercial risk.

2.3. Special leases

The leased asset is only designed (produced) for specific requirements of a particular lessee. After the initial lease period it usually can only be economically used by the lessee for whom it was first designed.

3. LEASES UNDER CIVIL LAW

Emerging in the late sixties, leasing has become a generally accepted term not only in an economic context but also as concerns German civil law. Although there is no general definition of a lease in German civil law, the provisions of the Civil Code regarding rental agreements apply to a large extent to lease contracts. In both the jurisdiction of the civil courts as well as in publications of jurisprudence, the importance of legal questions concerning leasing continues to increase.

3.1. The lease contract statutory provisions

A lease contract could be defined as an agreement between two parties, the lessor and the lessee, under which the lessor is obliged to provide the lessee with the leased asset directly from the supplier, who delivers the asset directly to the lessee. The lessee is obliged to pay the lease payments and to maintain the condition of the leased asset. He is responsible for any damage or deterioration of the leased asset and therefore receives any warranty payments that may arise.

In the German Civil Code special statutory provisions can be found regarding a general rental contract, which is quite different from the lease contract described above. For example, the renter of the German Civil Code rental contract is typically the owner of the rented asset, the recipient is viewed merely as a user and particular rental warranty provisions are specified.

Therefore the parties of a lease contract such as those described above usually deviate significantly from the statutory provisions, when adapting the Civil Code concept of rental. The modification of statutory rules by agreement does not cause serious problems regarding the application of the principle of „freedom of contract". However complications may arise if the lessor or the lessee use preformulated standard business contracts instead of individually formulated agreements. The Standard Business Conditions Law („Gesetz zur Regelung des Rechts der Allgemeinen Geschäftsbedingungen" AGBG) forbids certain deviations from the statutory provisions in order to protect the interest of the economically weaker party.

Under certain conditions, the lease contract can be considered to be a concealed sales contract which is governed by the rules of the Instalment Sales Law („Abzahlungsgesetz" AbzG). If the provisions of the lease contract include the full purchase price of the „leased" asset, combined with an obligation for the lessee to acquire the asset and the lease payments do not contain any element of interest, the „lease contract" will be deemed as an instalment sales contract. The AbzG requires a written contract and gives a buyer the right to withdraw from the contract. The provisions of the AbzG do not apply to commercial lease contracts.

3.2. Warranties

Following the general concept of a rental agreement as defined by the German Civil Code, the lessor must guarantee the proper functioning of the leased asset to the lessee and be responsible for all repairs and maintenance. As a rule these warranty provisions are usually altered by the parties of the lease contract so that warranty claims by the lessee can arise from both the generally accepted rules governing rentals and from specific agreements agreed upon between lessor and lessee.

3.2.1. Warranties preceding delivery

The lessor usually does not have any interest in the leased object itself, but merely finances the purchase price; the lessee therefore often negotiates directly with the supplier of the leased object. The supplier can therefore legally be considered as being employed by the lessor for the performance of his obligation. As a result the lessor will be liable for any damages caused by the supplier in favour of the lessee.

Furthermore, the lessor is liable for default or delivery delay unless these have been caused by the lessee himself. The warranty for default or delivery delay can be excluded either by individual agreement or by preformulated standard business conditions, however after having taken the restrictions under the AGBG into account.

3.2.2. Warranties during the term of the lease contract

As a rule, the general warranty rights of the lessee against the lessor differ from those specified under the German Civil Code for rental agreements. Under the lease contract specific sales warranty claims of the lessor against the supplier are assigned to the lessee. In the case of a faulty delivery the lessee is entitled to either demand a new delivery, a repair, a reduction of the purchase price, a rescission of the sale or to claim damages. If the sale which was concluded between the lessor and the supplier is rescinded, the lease contract between the lessor and the lessee becomes invalid and the lessee is freed from his obligation to make lease payments.

3.3. Termination of the lease contract

The typical finance lease contract, consisting of an initial lease term and an extension option, can be terminated in three different ways: through the lapse of time, notice or termination without notice.

3.3.1. Lapse of time

If the lease contract is concluded for a specific period of time, it will automatically terminate on the expiry date of the period. If the lessee does not exercise his option rights, he is obliged to return the leased asset and, should the return be delayed, to pay for damages.

3.3.2. Notice

During the initial lease term, termination with notice is not possible. If the initial term of the lease contract or the extension of the contract after the lapse of the initial lease term is unlimited, the lessee can terminate the lease contract after a period of notice. This period of notice depends on the length of the time interval between lease payments. The right to give notice can be excluded by both individual agreement and by standard business conditions.

3.3.3. Termination without notice

The lessee can terminate the lease contract without notice in the case of default or delivery delay, once the lessor has been issued a reminder and the default or delay has not been rectified. This right of termination exists only as long as the lessor is liable for the default or delivery delay.

The lessor has the right of termination without notice if the lessee uses the leased asset in a manner contrary to the terms of the lease contract or defaults on at least two consecutive lease payments. Further reasons for termination, such as bankruptcy of the lessee or execution levied upon the property of the lessee, can be documented in the lease contract by both individual agreement and by standard business conditions.

4. ACCOUNTING FOR LEASES

4.1. Economic ownership concept

The accounting treatment of leases in financial statements has been under discussion. There is no general legal definition of a lease and also no statutory accounting rules relating to leasing transactions. The accounting treatment must therefore rely on general accounting principles. In principle, the treatment for accounting purposes follows that for tax purposes.

Persons required to prepare financial statements (e.g. sole proprietor ships, partnerships and corporations) must ensure that the financial statements give a true and fair view of the situation of their business. To rely solely on the legal ownership of a leased asset, as defined in the lease contract, for the purposes of the financial statements would not fulfil this requirement. Instead, the Federal Tax Court has established that the economic point of view must also be considered for accounting purposes; each leasing contract must be reviewed carefully on the basis of the concept of economic ownership.

Appendix II contains a brief summary of the standard opinion of commentaries regarding the consequences of this requirement for the allocation of ownership of leased assets.

4.2. Economic ownership attributed to the lessor

There are principally two requirements for the lessor to be regarded as the economic owner of a leased asset:

- The lessee must not have the power to exclude the lessor from the use of the asset for substantial parts of its entire useful life.
- The lessor must retain a significant share in any future price increase affecting the asset.

Tax authorities have issued schematic regulations which cover many of the situations arising in practice.

4.2.1. Accounting rules for the lessor

The lessor must capitalise the leased asset at historical cost in his balance sheet. The asset can then be depreciated under the straight-line or the declining balance method (for details see section 5.1.1.1.). The monthly payments made by the lessee are recognised as current income.

Interest expense incurred in connection with a loan to finance the asset is disclosed in the profit and loss statement as interest expense.

A gain or loss on the disposal of the asset at the end of the lease period will be recognised as current income.

If future receivable lease payments are factorized, the discounted payments are shown as deferred income in the lessor's balance sheet. This entry must be reversed over the initial lease period (normally under the straight line method, although the method by which this reversal should be effected has not yet been finally determined).

For details of accounting entries see appendix IV.1.

4.2.2. Accounting rules for the lessee

The lessee does not capitalise the asset and reports no corresponding liability in his financial statements. A disclosure in the notes to the financial statements is required, however, if lease transactions are an important part of the lessee's business.

For details of accounting entries see appendix IV.2.

4.3. Economic ownership attributed to the lessee

If the above-mentioned requirements (section 4.2.) are not met, then the lessee is regarded as the economic owner of the leased asset and the lease contract as a conditional sale.

4.3.1. Accounting rules for the lessor

The lessor shows a receivable due from the lessee (instead of the asset) at historical cost of the leased asset, and therefore cannot claim any depreciation. The monthly lease payments are broken down into elements of income corresponding to interest and reimbursement of expense (plus a margin of profit, shown as revenue) and to redemption of the receivable.

4.3.2. Accounting rules for the lessee

The lessee must capitalise the leased asset at the historical cost to the lessor. However in most cases, since the lessee does not know the historical cost of the leased asset, he will in practice determine the market price of an equivalent asset and enter this into his financial statements. The asset can be depreciated under either the straight-line or the declining balance method. The lessee must also show a liability (discounted total future lease payments), equal to the value of the asset, which is reduced by a portion of the monthly lease payment.

Furthermore, the lessee must break down the monthly lease payments into interest expense and repayment of the liability. The relevant accounting entries are shown in appendix IV.2.

5. TAX ASPECTS OF LEASES

5.1. Domestic aspects of leases

The tax treatment of leases depends on the economic ownership of the leased assets, which is determined by case law of the Federal Tax Court and the subsequent detailed regulations from the Federal Ministry of Finance. See attached leasing rules in appendix III.

5.1.1. Corporate income tax

At present the corporate income tax rate is 50 % on income retained in the company and 36 % on income distributed as dividends. The corporate income tax rate for non-resident corporations (i.e. for permanent establishments in Germany, real estate income, etc.) is 46 %.

For corporate income tax purposes the tax basis is a company's income after trade tax on income and the addition of certain non-deductible items (e.g. cost of some business gifts, net asset tax, corporate income tax etc.).

Losses of up to DM 10,000,000 must be carried back to the two prior years. Any remaining balance can be carried forward indefinitely.

5.1.1.1. Depreciation

The economic owner, whether the lessor or the lessee, is entitled to claim the depreciation on the leased asset as a deductible expense. The asset must be capitalized at its historical cost. According to the depreciation tables issued by the German tax authorities, the asset can be depreciated under the straight-line or declining balance method over its useful life. However, the declining balance method is restricted to 3 times the amount of the straight-line method, with 30 % as a maximum. The useful life of used assets has to be re-estimated.

5.1.1.2. Taxation of lease payments

5.1.1.2.1. Treatment of current lease payments

If the lessor is considered the economic owner of the leased asset for tax purposes the monthly rental payments are treated as revenue in the respective fiscal year.

Any prepayments (balloon payments, front-end payments, etc.) made by the lessee have to be shown as deferred income in the financial statements of the lessor. The deferred income is reversed during the initial lease term.

Claims for future lease payments must not be reported as receivables because of their treatment as a pending transaction.

Should the lessee be considered the economic owner, the treatment is different since, for tax purposes, the lease contract is regarded as a conditional sale. The lease payment by the lessee must be split into repayment of the liability (principal) and interest payments. The interest payment is deductible as business expense, whereas the repayment of the principal only serves to reduce the corresponding reported liability.

5.1.1.2.2. Treatment of payments on exercise of an option

If the lease contract provides for an extension of the initial lease term, the treatment of the lease payments in later periods follows that described in section 5.1.1.2.1.

Should the lessor exercise a put option, the capital gain (difference between the book value at the time the option is exercised and the option price fixed at the time of conclusion of the lease contract) is recognised as ordinary income. The same applies to any capital loss incurred, which reduces other positive ordinary income. If a call option is exercised by the lessee, the call price represents acquisition costs for him. The used asset must be capitalised in the lessee's balance sheet at the call price and depreciated over its estimated remaining useful life.

5.1.2. Trade Tax (Gewerbesteuer)

This municipal tax is levied, at rates varying from city to city, by all municipalities in Germany. The tax bases are firstly the business profits and secondly the net assets of a company. Both are adjusted by certain add-back provisions and deductions.

5.1.2.1. Trade tax on income (Gewerbeertragsteuer)

„Long-term debt" for trade tax purposes refers to liabilities which are incurred either in order to establish, purchase or expand a business, a part thereof or an interest therein, or for a more than temporary increase in total capital. Liabilities whose maturity exceeds one year (12 months) will automatically qualify as long-term debt.

If the lessor is considered the economic owner of the leased asset, then 50 % of any interest payments arising from the „long-term" loan-financing (Dauerschulden) of the lease transaction are subject to trade tax on income. The lease payments reduce the profits of the lessee and so reduce his trade tax liability.

Should the lessee on the other hand be considered the economic owner, the interest on the discounted future lease obligations (=liability) is treated as long-term debt interest. If the lessor financed the leased asset by means of a loan and the lease term is longer than 6 years, the interest thereon will also be treated as long-term debt interest.

The income must be adjusted for trade tax on income purposes. It should be noted that trade tax on income is deductible from its own tax basis and also from the tax basis for corporate income tax purposes.

Losses incurred from 1985 onwards can be carried forward indefinitely.

5.1.2.2. Trade tax on capital (Gewerbekapitalsteuer)

An adjusted value of net assets is used as the basis for annual trade tax on capital.

If the lessor purchased the leased asset in a loan-financed transaction, then 50 % of his long-term debt is subject to annual trade tax on capital.

If the lessee is considered the economic owner, then the tax liability arises on 50 % of his long-term liability (in this case equivalent to the purchase price to the extent that it is still outstanding). The lessor's refinancing loan only qualifies as long-term debt when the lease term is more than 6 years.

Trade tax on capital is deductible both from the basis of trade tax on income and from the basis of corporate income tax.

5.1.2.3. Trade tax problems

A significant increase in overall trade tax liability results from the provisions for the adding back of 50 % of long-term debt to the basis for trade tax on capital, and of 50 % of interest expense to the basis for trade tax on income. The economic impact is that the refinancing expenses of the leasing company are increased significantly.

A possible solution in order to reduce the trade tax burden would be for the lessor to factorize future receivable lease payments to a German or foreign bank or another institution on a non-recourse basis. Banks conducting leasing transactions, however, might be forced to restructure their leasing business.

5.1.3. Value added tax (Umsatzsteuer)

As in other EEC countries a value added tax (VAT) is imposed in Germany. In general, it represents no overall cost burden for businessmen and entrepreneurs, instead private individuals and VAT-exempted industries (generally banks, insurance companies, etc.) bear the whole tax burden.

The imposition of VAT depends on which contract party is regarded as the economic owner of the leased asset. If the lessor is the economic owner, the leasing contract is treated as a rental agreement for VAT purposes and 14 % VAT is levied on the monthly lease payments. A call or put option exercised after the initial lease term will also be subject to 14 % VAT. If the lessee is fully-entitled to claim the paid VAT (input VAT), the VAT included in the lease payments will be refunded by the tax authorities.

If on the other hand the lessee is regarded as the economic owner, the lease contract is treated as a conditional sale for VAT purposes. The discounted value of the instalments to be paid, including the amount of any final purchase price or any instalments to be paid after the expiry of the initial lease term, will immediately be subject to 14 % VAT. The lessee will be entitled to claim input VAT if he is an entrepreneur (except for VAT-exempted industries, e.g. banks, insurance companies, etc.).

Each company is obliged to prepare monthly VAT returns. These are then summarised in the annual VAT return.

5.1.4. Net asset tax (Vermögensteuer)

The net assets of a corporate entity are subject to an annual German net asset tax at 0.6 %. Since only 75 % of net business assets are subject to the tax, the effective annual tax rate is 0.45 % on total net assets. Individuals are subject to net asset tax at 0.5 % on their worldwide assets. Each individual is entitled to claim a tax-free allowance of DM 70,000.

The net asset tax is not deductible for corporate income tax and trade tax on income purposes.

Only the economic owner of the leased asset is subject to net asset tax on the basis of the asset's fair market value. If the lessee is considered the economic owner he can deduct the corresponding liability against the value of the leased asset. The lessor has to show the value of the future lease payments as a receivable. This receivable therefore becomes subject to net asset tax. However, the corresponding financing costs are deductible for net asset tax purposes.

5.2. International tax aspects of leases

Cross-border leasing has become prominent due to the tax advantages potentially available from the differing treatments of a lease contract under two or more jurisdictions („double dipping"). Furthermore, the creation of the internal European market in 1992 is likely to encourage increasing competition once the barriers for such international agreements are reduced. As a result, leasing companies have begun to look for more favourable financing methods. These financing techniques are largely developed by international investment banking firms, which take advantage of special financial centres or special structures to establish companies, holding entities etc. in different countries.

5.2.1. Classification of lease payments

If two parties intend to conclude a cross-border lease contract, the treatment of the lease payments in both the jurisdictions must be taken into consideration. Assuming the existance of a tax treaty between Germany and the respective country, it will have to be determined whether the lease payments qualify under the royalty article or some other income article of the treaty. In most of Germany's double tax treaties, „royalties" include the right to use industrial, scientific or commercial equipment. Most of these treaties provide for the exemption of royalties from withholding tax. The following tax treaties provide for a reduction/exemption of withholding taxes:

Country	Tax rate
Austria	0
Belgium	0
France	0
Great Britain	0
Italy	0
Japan	10/0
Luxembourg [1])	0
Netherlands	0
Switzerland	0
USA	0

5.2.2. Taxation of lease payments

5.2.2.1. Taxation of lease payments to foreign lessors

If a foreign lessor is treated as the economic owner of the leased asset, lease payments made by a German lessee are treated as rental payments for German domestic tax purposes and the gross amount of the payments may be liable to German withholding tax on royalties (see section 5.2.1.).

Generally, if the lessor does not have a permanent establishment in Germany, the lease payments will be treated either as royalties or as other income under the relevant double tax treaty. In the case of lease payments qualifying as other income under a treaty, the right of taxation is assigned to the country where the foreign lessor is established and no German withholding tax will be payable. Payments qualifying as royalties may be treaty exempted from withholding tax or only subject to reduced treaty rates. In all other cases the lessee is obliged to withhold 25 % withholding tax on behalf of the foreign lessor.

[1]) Tax exempt holding companies are not subject to the double tax treaty.

Lease payments made by the lessee are deductible as business expense for corporate income tax purposes. However, for trade tax on income purposes 50 % of the lease payments are added back. For trade tax on capital purposes the value of the leased asset, in addition, is subject to this tax.

Exemption from German taxation is only available, when under the treaty the lessor is not deemed to have a permanent establishment in Germany to which the lease transaction is deemed to be allocated. Usually a permanent establishment will not be assumed in the case of a single cross-border lease transaction and, subject to the provisions of the royalty article, the lease payments will be subject to 25 % German withholding tax, if no treaty relief is available.

However, if the lessor does have a permanent establishment in Germany, all future lease payments, less depreciation and other expense, will be attributed to the permanent establishment and subject to approximately 19.4 % trade tax (1990 Frankfurt tax rate) and 46 % corporate income tax.

If the German lessee is treated as the economic owner of the leased asset, the lease is deemed to be a conditional sale under German tax law. The income derived by the foreign lessor from the assumed instalment sale will not be subject to German tax, unless it is attributable to a permanent establishment maintained by the foreign lessor in Germany. This applies under domestic law as well as under a double taxation treaty.

5.2.2.2. Taxation of lease payments to German lessors

A German resident lessor is subject to an unlimited German tax liability on his worldwide income. If he is considered the economic owner of the leased asset, foreign withholding tax is in principle creditable, and depreciation and other expenses are deductible in order to reduce the taxable income.

If, on the other hand, the foreign lessee is treated as the economic owner, the German lessor will be treated as if he has sold the asset under a conditional sales contract. Any income derived from the assumed sale will be subject to German taxation.

5.2.3. Anti-avoidance rules

The German tax laws do contain provisions which apply to cases where the routing of lease payments through intermediate companies established either in tax haven countries or in countries with a double tax treaty with Germany are structured without any economic substance or reasoning behind the structure („treaty shopping"). When no economic substance can be evidenced the tax benefits from the lease transactions will be disregarded.

6. SPECIAL TAX ASPECTS OF LEASES

6.1. Real estate leases

6.1.1. The German real estate leasing market

Real estate leases are now a recognised financing instrument in all parts of the German economy, especially in connection with sale-and-lease-back transactions (see section 6.2.). Today real estate leases should always be taken into consideration when determining the optimum financing of a building. However, the real estate leasing market made up only 3.5 % of total business real estate investments in Germany in 1987; only 9 % of all lease investments in that year were made in real estate.

In general, real estate leases are specifically designed for the lessee to incorporate his special conditions or requirements. Furthermore the economic use by the lessee must be maintained for a longer period than the initial lease period. The leased real estate has a long useful life and high initial investment costs.

Usually, each real estate asset is held by a separate entity, in the form of a GmbH or a partnership (e.g. a GmbH & Co. KG). These entities themselves are held by a real estate leasing company which acts as a holding company and takes over the administration of the separate entities in return for a fee. The advantages of this structure for the leasing company are that the commercial risk attached to each real estate asset can be separately assessed, any transactions regarding a single asset need not have any direct effect on the company's other holdings, and when the company's activities involve leasing solely its own real estate, the basis for Trade Tax on Income is reduced by the amount of its yields therefrom.

6.1.2. Types of real estate leasing contracts

The large number of different real estate lease contracts illustrate their flexiblity in meeting the varied requirements of the lessor and lessee. However, most contracts are based on one of three principal types: full pay out, non-full pay out, and lease prepayment contracts.

6.1.2.1. Full pay out leases

In this model, the lease payments made during the initial lease term fully amortise the total value of the leased asset including all financing, administrative and depreciation costs incurred by the lessor.

This model is used comparatively rarely, not least of all because the lease payments during the initial lease term are relatively high. However the model can still be advantageous if the chances of leasing the asset to a third party on expiry of the initial lease term are considered to be very low, or if the valuation of the asset proves to be particulary difficult or even impossible.

6.1.2.2. Non-full pay out leases

The non-full pay out model is the most frequently used method today. Unlike the full pay out model, the total value of the leased asset is not amortised over the initial lease term. As a result the lease payments are lower than under a full pay out lease and the lessor continues to bear some element of commercial risk on expiry of the initial lease term. Thus, the non full pay out lease tends to be more attractive to the lessee.

The lessor will retain the ownership of the real estate upon expiry of the initial lease term, and will have to consider the commercial risk that he will continue to bear.

6.1.2.3. Prepayment leases

The prepayment lease is a particular type of non-full pay out lease. During the initial lease term the lessor receives prepaid lease payments from the lessee, so that on expiry of the initial lease term the total prepaid lease payments are equal to the residual book value of the leased real estate.

Should the lessor sell the asset to a third party on expiry of the initial lease term, the lessee is entitled to a share in the profit (or loss) on the sale, over and above the amount of his prepaid expense. The loan contract must specify the amount payable by the lessor to the lessee if the lessor should enter into a lease contract with a third party on expiry of the initial lease term.

6.1.3. Taxation of real estate leases

The economic ownership concept (as described in section 4.) also applies to real estate leases. Appendix II.2. contains a summary of rules governing the allocation of real estate assets between the lessor and the lessee.

If the lessor is considered the economic owner of the leased asset, prepayments entered by the lessor and the lessee are recorded as deferred income and prepaid expense respectively for the purposes of the financial statements. On exercise of a purchase or extension option, these entries will be reversed either at the time of sale or over the term of the extension.

Lease payments are recognised by the lessor as ordinary income. If the asset is a new building, he is entitled to deduct depreciation expense under either the straight-line or declining balance method.

Under certain preconditions special trade tax rules become applicable, resulting in a lower trade tax burden.

In general the lease payments are not subject to German value added tax. However, the lessor has the possibility to opt for taxation in order to claim the input VAT as a credit and therefore reduce the financing costs of the construction.

6.2. Sale and leaseback transactions

6.2.1. Purpose of the transaction

Sale-and-leaseback transactions are typically used when a company requires additional funds (e.g. for business expansion plans, to offset losses or to avoid thin capitalisation) and when the sale of assets is considered to be preferable to an increase in equity or debt, yet these assets are still required for the company's business operations.

Under sale and leaseback transactions an asset is sold to another party who then leases the asset back to the seller. The lease contract often gives the seller a call option in respect of the asset. The seller will usually recognise a gain from the transaction because the fair market value of assets is usually higher than the book value reported in the financial statements due to hidden reserves.

6.2.2. Tax treatment of sale and leaseback transactions

Under the assumption that the sale price realised is higher than the residual book value of the asset, the lessee (seller) is taxable on the gain (difference between residual book value and fair market value) treated as ordinary income. This tax liability could similarly be offset through lease payments in the following years if not fully or partially offset by any existing loss-carry forwards.

Another possibility to at least partly avoid an increased tax liability is to create a reinvestment reserve (Sec. 6b German Income Tax Law).

Under a sale and leaseback agreement the general principles regarding economic ownership apply. The transaction will only be advantageous for the lessee if he has other profitable investment opportunities and if the tax liability of the gain on the sale can be reduced (e.g. by the creation of a reinvestment reserve).

In principle, the German tax authorities accept sale and leaseback transactions provided economic substance is demonstrated.

6.3. Tax incentives for leasing in West-Berlin

West-Berlin leasing companies may take advantage of considerable tax incentives which can be categorized into incentives for the lessor and incentives in respect of the leased asset itself.

However, at the moment it is not clear whether the tax incentives will be maintained for the future or if they will be abolished. After the German federal elections in December 1990, the German parliament may reconsider the adequacy of respective subsidies/incentives.

6.3.1. Incentives for the leasing company

Companies and branches are entitled to a tax free investment subsidy for the acquisition or construction of new movable fixed assets and for certain immovable fixed assets, provided that the assets remain in Berlin branch for at least 3 years and are located in Berlin.

The subsidies are based on acquisition or manufacturing costs and do not reduce the tax basis for depreciation purposes of the asset.

These subsidies can be applied to the assets acquired by leasing companies to the extent that the leasing company becomes the economic owner of the asset.

A system of accelerated depreciation applies to depreciable movable fixed assets and to certain immovable fixed assets in cases where the Berlin leasing company becomes the economic owner of the asset. Such assets may be depreciated either in the year of acquisition/construction or over a period of 4 years, to a net book value of 25 %.

Leasing companies may take advantage of the following low or reduced tax rates:

a) Trade tax on income and capital

The Berlin trade tax rate is approximately 50 % lower than rates applied in other large German cities. The current rate in Berlin is 9.1 %, as compared to a rate of 19.4 % in Frankfurt.

b) Corporate income tax

The current Berlin corporate income tax rate is 38.75 %. This represents a 22.5 % reduction of the 50 % rate which applies to all other parts of West Germany.

c) Individual income tax

The Berlin individual income tax rate with a maximum of 37.1 % is 30 % lower than the rates applying to other areas of West Germany where a maximum rate of 53 % is currently in force.

6.3.2. Incentives applying to the leased asset

VAT preferences are available between 2 % and 10 %, depending upon certain conditions.

A tax free investment subsidy is granted for movable fixed assets leased within Berlin. Where the lessee becomes the economic owner of the asset, the subsidy may be claimed by the lessee when the asset remains in Berlin.

The Berlin accelerated depreciation provisions (see 6.3.1.) may be applied by the economic owner to leased movable fixed assets located in Berlin. These provisions may only be applied to immovable fixed assets when the assets are used by their economic owner.

INDEX OF THE APPENDICES

IV. Journal entries (accounting)

Fig 1: German leasing market in comparison to other European countries (estimated total acquisition value of all leased assets, excluding real estate, billion DM)

Country	1987	1988*	Change (%)
FRG	97,779	107,560	+10.0
Great Britain	91,127	100,240	+10.0
France	31,433	37,720	+20.0
Spain	12,659	18,990	+50.0
Sweden	9,293	10,220	+10.0
Netherlands	4,721	4,900	+3.8
Belgium	3,908	4,880	+24.9
Switzerland	3,295	3,950	+19.9
Denmark	2,776	3,610	+30.0
Norway	3,055	3,115	+2.0

*: estimated Source: Leaseurope

Fig. 2: Leasing investment in Germany
(Total: billion DM)

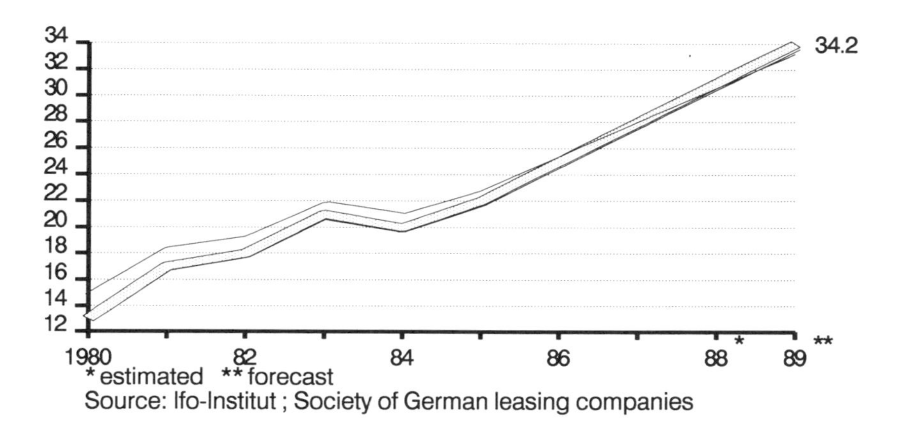

* estimated ** forecast
Source: Ifo-Institut ; Society of German leasing companies

Fig. 3: Leasing investment as a proportion of total investment in Germany

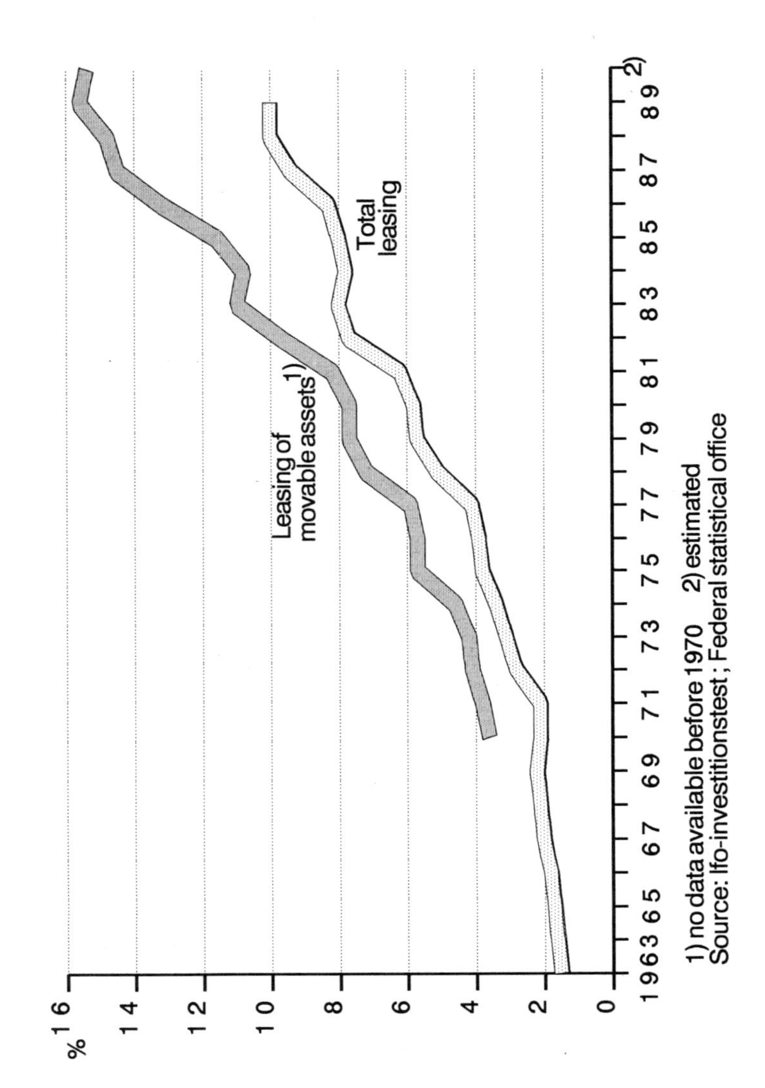

1) no data available before 1970 2) estimated
Source: Ifo-investitionstest; Federal statistical office

Fig. 4a : Leasing investment as a proportion of total business investment in Germany

	1981	1982	1983	1984	1985	1986	1987 [b]	1988 [b]
Total business investment (million DM) [a]	239,030	232,400	241,920	247,620	264,070	280,770	292,480	311,900
Change on previous year (%)	+0.1	-2.8	+4.1	+2.4	+6.6	+6.3	+4.2	+6.6
Compare:								
Leasing investment (million DM)	16,450	17,250	20,190	19,400	21,350	24,530	28,280	31,100
Change on previous year (%)	+24.9	+4.9	+17.0	-3.9	+10.1	+14.9	+15.3	+10.0
Leasing investment as a percentage of total business investment [c]	6.9	7.4	8.3	7.8	8.1	8.7	9.7	10.0

a) new buildings and equipment b) estimated c) leasing by institutions and manufacturers

Source: Ifo-Institut, Ifo Institutionstest Anlagevermietung; Federal statistical office

Fig 4b : Leasing of movable assets and of real estate in Germany

	1982	1983	1984	1985	1986	1987 [a]	1988 [a]
Total business equipment investment (new equipment) in million DM	129,580	140,490	143,000	159,670	167,830	175,860	187,300
Leasing investment in movable assets (including manufacturers' leasing) in million DM	12,170	15,470	15,450	18,570	22,150	25,780	28,360
Leasing of movable assets as a percentage of total business equipment investment	9.4	11.0	10.8	11.6	13.2	14.7	15.1
Commercial construction investment in million DM [b]	57,820	60,170	63,840	63,770	70,450	70,990	76,500
Real estate leasing in million DM	5,100	4,720	3,950	2,780	2,380	2,500	2,740
Real estate leasing as a percentage of commercial construction investment in million DM	8.8	7.8	6.2	4.4	3.4	3.5	3.6

a) estimated b) total commercial construction investment excluding private housing, public sector investment and non-profitmaking organisations.

Source: Ifo-Investitionstest Anlagenvermietung ; Federal statistical office

Fig.5: Distribution of leasing investments in Germany in 1988

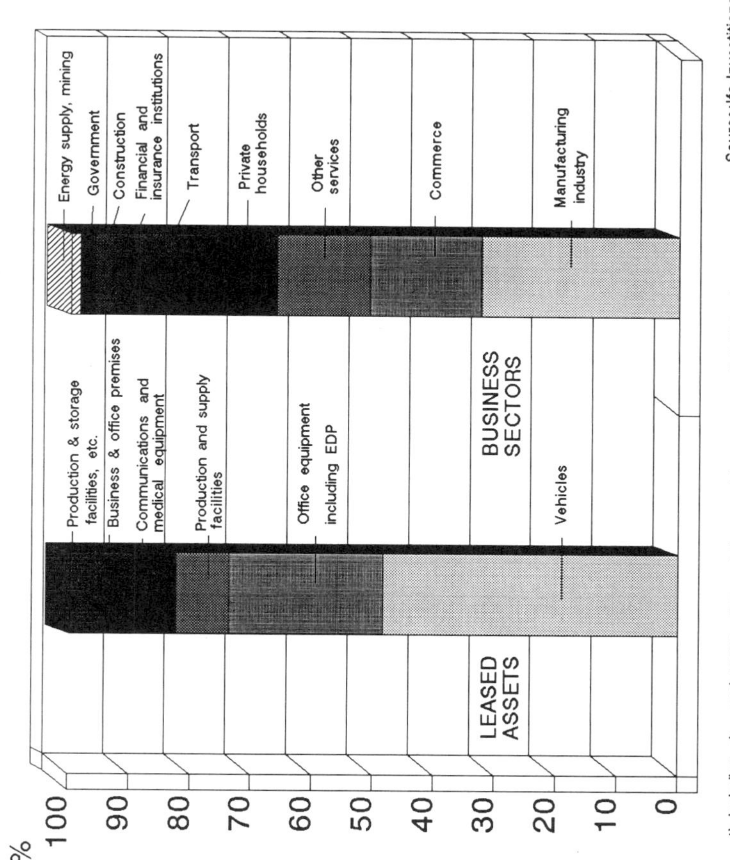

1) including air - and water - transportation, containers, cranes, fork-lift trucks,etc
2) including agriculture and foresty
3) including non - profitmaking organisations

Source: Ifo-Investitionstest; Ifo-Institut für Wirtschaftsforschung, München

1. LEASES OF MOVABLE ASSETS

1. 1 FULL PAY OUT CONTRACTS

ALLOCATION OF LEASED ASSET TO LESSEE, IF

1. SPECIAL LEASING	
2. INITIAL LEASE TERM (ILT)	$< 40\ \%$ or $> 90\ \%$ of normal useful life
3. CALL OPTION	ILT $\geq 40\ \%$ and $\leq 90\ \%$ of normal useful life, but purchase price $<$ book value determined by the straight-line depreciation method or fair market value (whichever is lower)
4. EXTENSION OPTION	ILT $\geq 40\ \%$ and $\leq 90\ \%$ of normal useful life, but remaining lease payments for period of extension $<$ straight-line depreciation based on historical cost or fair market value (whichever is lower) under the consideration of the remaining useful life.

1.2 NON-FULL PAY OUT CONTRACTS

TYPE OF CONTRACT	ALLOCATION TO
1. ILT $\geq 40\ \%$ and $\leq 90\ \%$ of normal useful life and lessor has put option lessee has no call option	Lessor

2. ILT $\geqslant$ 40 % and $\leqslant$ 90 % of normal useful life and on subsequent sale any loss is borne by lessee while any profit is shared between lessor and lessee. When lessor receives	
$\geqslant$ 25 % of profit	Lessor
$<$ 25 % of profit	Lessee
3. ILT $\geqslant$ 40 % and $\leqslant$ 90 % of normal useful life and lessee has option to cancel at any time after expiry of ILT. Lessee is obliged to make a final payment equivalent to the remaining amortisation. This payment is reduced by 90 % of the price realised by the lessor on sale of the asset.	Lessor

2. REAL ESTATE LEASES

TYPE OF CONTRACT	ALLOCATION TO
1. SPECIAL LEASE	Lessee
2. GROUND	
- finance lease without options	Lessor
- finance lease with call option	Lessee, if building also allocated to lessee
- finance lease with extension option	Lessor
3. BUILDING LEASE	
-ILT < 40 % and > 90 % of normal useful life of building or of corresponding shorter ground lease term	Lessee

-ILT $\geqslant$40 % and $\leqslant$ 90 % of normal useful life and	
no options	Lessor
call option, but price must be at least equal to residual book value after ILT (straight line depreciation) plus lower than book or fair market value of the ground	Lessor
extension option, but lease payments must be at least 75 % of rental payments for a comparable building	Lessor
4. ALL OTHER CASES	Lessee

1. Leasing versus conditional sale (Full pay out leases)

1.1. General

Leasing contracts concluded after April 23, 1970 are subject to the principles of the Supreme Tax Court ruling of January 26, 1970 which basically has the following contents:

1.1.1. Whether a lease is regarded as a conditional sale is determined on the basis of economic reality as opposed to the leasing contract's strictly legal provisions.

1.1.2. Irrespective of the wording of the leasing contract, a conditional sale is assumed if certain characteristics prevail.

1.1.3. A conditional sale is assumed

1.1.3.1. If the normal useful life of the asset is considerably longer than the initial lease term provided for in the contract, and if the lessee has the right to opt either for purchase or for an extension of the lease at considerable lower cost than that incurred in a regular purchase or rental/lease contract; or

1.1.3.2. in the absence of an option, if the useful life of the asset and the initial lease term are about equal; or

1.1.3.3. in the absence of 1.3.1. and 1.3.2. above, if the leased asset fits the specific needs of the lessee only and if only the latter can use it economically after the expiry of the initial lease term.

1.2. „Finance Leasing“

1.2.1. The principles of the above court ruling are only applicable to so-called „Finance Leasing“. The release gives the following criteria for the determination of „Finance Leasing“.

1.2.1.1. The contract has been concluded for a certain period of time during which it cannot be cancelled. This is the so-called initial lease term.

1.2.1.2. The lessee's lease payments during the initital lease term at least equal the lessor's total costs, including financing costs.

1.3. Criteria for the qualification of the finance leasing contract concerning movable fixed assets as a leasing contract or as a conditional sales contract.

1.3.1. Lease contracts without purchase or extension options

1.3.1.1. Allocation to the lessor
if the initial lease term is at least 40 % and not more than 90 % of the normal useful life.

1.3.1.2. Allocation to the lessee
if the initial lease term is less than 40 % or more than 90 % of the normal useful life as per official depreciation tables.

1.3.2. Lease contracts with purchase options

1.3.2.1. Allocation to the lessor

- if the initial lease term is at least 40 % and not more than 90 % of the useful life of the leased asset, and
- if the purchase price payable on exercise of the option is not less than the book value of the asset (determined by applying straight-line depreciation according to the official depreciation tables) or the fair market value, whichever is lower.

1.3.2.2. Allocation to the lessee

- if the initial lease term is less than 40 % or more than 90 % of the normal useful life, or

- if the initial lease term is within that interval and the purchase price is less than the book value of the asset (after straight-line depreciation in accordance with the official depreciation tables) or the fair market value, whichever is lower.

If the purchase option is exercised and the purchase price is determined during or after the end of the initial lease term, the above principles apply accordingly. Assessment notices issued, if any, have to be corrected.

1.3.3. Leasing contracts with extension options

The lessee is entitled to extend the contract for a certain period of time or indefinitely after the end of the initial lease term, which is normally shorter than the useful life of the asset.

Lease contracts without an extension option, but with a clause providing for an automatic extension at the end of the initial lease term if neither of the two parties gives notice, are principally to be treated for tax purposes in the same manner as lease contracts with an extension option. An exception applies if the lessor can prove that numerous lease contracts concerning assets of the same kind have been terminated within a period of 90 % of the useful life.

1.3.3.1. Allocation to the lessor

- if the initial lease term is at least 40 % and not more than 90 % of the normal useful life of the leased asset, and

- if the total lease payments after that time at least equal the depreciation for the remaining useful life, determined according to the official depreciation tables. The basis of such depreciation is the book value (arrived at by straight-line depreciation according to the official depreciation tables) or the fair market value, whichever is lower.

1.3.3.2. Allocation to the lessee

- If the initial lease term is within than 40 % or more than 90 % of the normal useful life of the leased asset, or
- if the initial lease term is within that interval and the total lease payments after that time are less than depreciation for the remaining useful life, determined according to the official depreciation tables. The basis of such depreciation is the book value (arrived at by straight-line depreciation according to the official depreciation table) or the fair market value, whichever is lower.
- if the lease payments for the extension period are determined or modified during or after the initial lease term, the same principles apply accordingly.

1.3.4. Contracts with regard to so-called „special leasing"

These are contracts referring to assets specifically designed for and adapted to the circumstances of the lessee. After the end of the initial lease term these assets can normally be used by the lessee only. Such contracts may or may not include an option.

Irrespective of the relationship between the initial lease term and the useful life, and irrespective of option clauses, the assets are allocable to the lessee.

1.4. Criteria for the qualification of a finance leasing contract concerning immovable assets as a leasing contract or a conditional sales contract.

In the case of finance leasing contracts regarding immovable assets, buildings and land are treated differently.

1.4.1. Allocation of a building

1.4.1.1. Lease contracts without purchase or extension option

- Allocation to the lessor

If the initial lease term is at least 40 % and not more than 90 % of the normal useful life (as per official depreciation tables).

- Allocation to the lessee

If the initial lease term is less than 40 % or more than 90 % of the normal useful life.

1.4.1.2. Lease contracts with purchase options

- Allocation to the lessor

If the initial lease term is at least 40 % and not more than 90 % of the useful life of the leased asset, and the purchase price payable on exercise of the option is not less than the book value of the asset (determined by applying straight-line depreciation according to the official depreciation tables) plus the book value of the land, or the total market value at the time of sale, whichever is lower.

- Allocation to the lessee

If the initial lease term is less than 40 % or more than 90 % of the normal useful life, or if the initial lease term is within this interval and the purchase price, if the option is exercised, at least equals the book value or market value at that time, whichever is lower.

If the purchase option is exercised and the purchase price is determined during or after the end of the initial lease term, the above principles apply accordingly. Issued assessment notices, if any, have to be corrected.

1.4.1.3. Leasing contracts with extension option

- Allocation to the lessor

If the initial lease term is at least 40 % and not more than 90 % of the normal useful life of the leased asset and if the future lease payments are more than 75 % of those for an equivalent asset.

- Allocation to the lessee

If the initial lease term is less than 40 % or more than 90 % of the normal useful life of the leased asset, or if the initial lease term is within this interval and the furture lease payments do not exceed 75 % of those for an equivalent asset.

1.4.2. Allocation of land

1.4.2.1. Lease contracts without purchase or extension options
Allocation to the lessor

1.4.2.2. Lease contracts with purchase options

- Allocation to the lessor

If the building is allocable to the lessor according to 4.1.

- Allocation to the lesseee

If the building is allocable to the lessee according to 4.1.

1.4.2.3. Lease contracts with extension options

Allocation to the lessor

1.5. Tax treatment of a lease and a conditional sale

1.5.1. Lease contracts

1.5.1.1. Lessee
The lease payments are treated as business expenses.

1.5.1.2. Lessor
The lessor has to capitalise the assets at historical cost. Depreciation has to be applied in accordance with the official depreciation tables. The lease payments are treated as income of the lessor.

1.5.2. Conditional sale

1.5.2.1. Lessee
The lessee must capitalize the assets on the basis of the historical cost which the lessor used to fix the rent, plus any additional costs not included in the rent.

The lessee is entitled to depreciate the asset over its normal useful life.

The lessee has to show a liability in his financial statements equal to the value of the asset as stated, minus any costs not included in the lease payments.

The lease payments must be broken down into interest and expense on the one hand and payment of principal on the other hand. Of course, as time elapses the former portion will decrease while the latter will increase.

Interest and costs are deductible business expenses, whereas the payment of principal must be applied against the respective liability.

1.5.2.2. Lessor

The lessor's financial statements show a receivable amounting to that portion of the lease payments which represents the payment of principal. Generally this amount will be equal to the corresponding liability on the lessee's books.

2. Non full pay out leases (Allocation of a leased asset to the lessor Federal Minister of Finance's ruling of December 22, 1975)

2.1. The forms of contract treated here have in common an initial lease term (during which the contract may not be rescinded) of between 40 % and 90 % of normal useful life. The rent paid during this period only partially covers the historical cost (including ancillary cost such as cost of financing) incurred by the lessor for the asset. Consequently, it is not a case of „finance leasing" as this term is used in the Federal Minister of Finance's ruling of April 19, 1971 regarding the income tax treatment of lease contracts on movable assets, and the question to whom the asset is to be allocated must be settled in the light of general principles.

2.2. We have reached the following conclusions regarding the above question:

a) If the lessor has a put option and the lessee does not have a call option:

In these contracts, the lessee is obliged, if the lessor so requires, at the end of the basic period of lease, to buy the asset at a price agreed when the lease contract was concluded. He may not demand to buy the asset.

In such cases, the lessee bears the risk that the asset may diminish in value, since he is obliged to buy it at the price previously fixed, if the lessor exercises his option, although a similar asset would cost less. The lessor, on the other hand, enjoys the opportunity of an increase in value, since he need not exercise his put option, but may instead sell the asset at the current market price, if higher.

Under these circumstances, the lessee cannot be regarded as the owner of the asset in an economic sense.

b) If lessor and lessee share the profit on a subsequent sale:

At the end of the initial lease term, the lessor sells the asset leased. If the price realised is less than the remaining amortization (i.e. that portion of the lessor's total cost not covered by the rent paid), the difference is to be borne by the lessee. If the price realised is higher than the remaining amortization, the difference is divided between the parties, the lessor receiving 25 % and the lessee 75 %.

This agreement that the lessor shall receive 25 % of any profit on the subsequent sale means that he shares to a material extent in any increase in value of the leased asset. As a result, the asset is to be assigned to him.

The lessor's share in any increase in value is immaterial, on the other hand, if he is to receive less than 25 % of any profit. In such cases, the asset is to be assigned to the lessee.

c) If the lessee may rescind the contract and credit the profit realised on subsequent sale to his final payment:

The lessee may rescind the leasing agreement at any time once the initial lease term, which amounts to 40 % of the normal useful life of the leased asset, has expired, in which case he is obliged to make a final payment equivalent to the remaining amortization as defined above. This payment is reduced by 90 % of the price realised by the lessor on

selling the asset. Where 90 % of the profit on the sale of the asset exceeds the remaining amortization then the lessee's final payment is reduced to nil, but the lessor retains the excess profit.
In such cases, the lessor enjoys any increase in value of the leased asset, and is consequently the owner of the asset in an economic as well as a legal sense.
The above has general validity, but may be overridden by special provisions in actual contracts.

3. Accounting for a lease contract by the lessor (Federal Minister of Finance's ruling of May 13, 1980)

My rulings of April 19, 1971 and March 21, 1972 require the lessor if he is obliged to reflect the leased asset in his financial statements to do so at historical cost. The rental payments are income. If the leased asset is movable and depreciable, the lessor may deduct depreciation amounts depending on its normal useful life.
The following questions have arisen in this connection:

a) Can the entire amount of rental payments agreed be capitalized as „rental accounts payable" (thus increasing the lessor's income immediately) and subsequently depreciated according to the standard linear method, and a corresponding liability („services to be rendered") be accrued and subsequently reduced according to the graduated calculation of interest method (i.e. more slowly than the standard linear method)?
b) Can a loss, which is expected from the subsequent sale of the leased asset, be accrued for in the lessor's balance, or can it justify increased depreciation amounts?
On consulation with the states' senior tax authorities, my position as regards these questions is as follows:

1) Accounting for rental payments

If the asset leased is allocated to the lessor, then the lease contract has been recognized as such. A lease contract is a transaction not yet settled and as such may not be reflected in a balance sheet. Therefore, rental payment not yet due and services to be rendered may not appear in the balance sheet.

2) Provisions for expected loss

Depreciation amounts are calculated just as the rental payments are on the basis of the normal life of the asset as listed in the official depreciation schedules. Higher amounts are not permitted.

An accrual for expected loss requires the existence of a liability. Since the sales contract in the cases in question has not yet been concluded, this requirement is not fulfilled, and an accrual is not permitted.

4. Factoring of lease receivables

Release from the Finance Minister of Nordrhein-Westfalen from February 13, 1980.

Leasing companies, which, as lessors, are deemed to be the equitable owners of the leased object, have adopted the practice of assigning individual claims against the lessee arising from the leasing agreement to third parties (e.g. a bank) in return for consideration (sale of receivables).

The lessor continues to be bound to give up the use of the leased object to the lessee. The buyer of the receivable has the right to claim the receivable. The leasing company does not guarantee the ability of the lessee to pay, nor is it obliged to repurchase the claim in the case of the receivable being uncollectable. The leasing company is liable merely for the legal existence of the receivable and its unencumbrance from defences, not only at the time of sale, but also for the duration of the leasing agreement.

Due to this guarantee the bank has a claim of recourse against the lessor if the lessee can avoid payment of the leasing installment due to nonfulfillment of the obligations arising under the leasing agreement on the part of the lessor. If the lessee becomes unable to pay and thus terminates the leasing agreement prematurely, then the proceeds arising from the leasing object will be divided between the leasing company and the credit institution taking into consideration the receivables which have been lost.

The obligation to surrender the use of the leasing object to the lessee, which remains with the lessor after the sale of the receivables, should be shown as a debit-item in the schedule of assets. In the tax balance sheet, because of the sale of the receivables, a deferred income item should be set up according to § 5 para. 3 No. 2 EStG (Income Tax Act) (Rent advance payments) for the cash received, which according to part. 34 Capital Tax Directives, can also be applied for the capital taxation.

For the determination of the trade capital, the obligation to surrender the use of the leasing object is not to be re-added to the assessed value of the commercial business according to § 12 para. 2 No. 1 GewStG (Trade Tax Act). The conditions stipulated in § 8 No. 1 GewStG for the assumption of a long-term debt are not fulfilled in the given facts. The obligation of the owner of a thing to surrender its use, does not serve to strenghten his business capital.

5. Ruling of the Federal Minister of Finance concerning income tax treatment of finance leases

The apportionment of the leasing installments into interest and cost portions as well as into repayment portions.

From December 13, 1973 IV B2 S. 2170 94/73

With reference to the results of discussions with the income tax experts of the highest finance authorities of the individual states, I comment as follows on the question of the apportionment of leasing installments into interest and cost portions and into a repayment portion:

According to my circular from March 19, 1973 IV B2 S. 217 4/73 in those cases where the leasing object is attributed to the lessee, the interest and cost portions contained in the leasing installments can be calculated by taking the total amount of the consideration to be paid by the lessee prior to and during the basic leasing period, and reducing this amount by the acquisition or production costs incurred by the lessor, which is the basis of calculating the leasing installments. By the apportionment of the individual installments it should be taken into consideration that due to the continuous amortization, the interest portion is reduced and the repayment portion is increased.

The lessee may calculate the interest and cost portions contained in the individual leasing installments in such a way that he reduces the total leasing installments falling within the financial year by the difference between the cash value of the liability towards the lessor at the beginning of the financial year and that at the end. The acquisition and production costs capitalized by the lessee, with the exception of those acquisition and production costs of the lessee not taken into account in the leasing installments, are to be taken as the cash value of the liability at the time of its coming into existence.

As the interest portion by the cash value comparison method can only be calculated with the assistance of the interest tables, there are no objections to calculating the interest portion by way of the interest graduation method in view of comparison of the cash values. The interest graduation method also assumes that the interest portion will continually decrease due to the continuous amortization.

By the interest graduation method, the interest and cost portions of a leasing installment can be calculated using the following formula:

Sum of interest and cost portions of all leasing installments

.... x Number of remaining installments + 1

Sum of numerical series of all installments

In this case the total amount of the interest and cost portions of all leasing installments is the difference between the total of all leasing installments on the one side, and the acquisition or production costs incurred for the leasing object, which were the basis of calculating the leasing installments, on the other side.

The total amount of the interest and cost portions is to be calculated and treated uninformly. It is not permissible to calculate the cost portions separately and to apportion them in equal accrual amounts over the duration of the leasing period (linear).

The sum of the numerical row of all installments is calculated using the formula for a finite arithmetical series:

$$Sn = \frac{n}{2} (gl + gn)$$

Symbols:

n = Total number of installments to be paid

gl = 1

gn = Number of installments still to be paid

If the lessee must make a one-off special payment at the beginning of the leasing agreement, then this is to be treated as a premium and booked on the assets side by the lessee, to be apportioned over the period of the lease term. The apportionment is to be carried out corresponding to the apportionment of the interest and cost portions, as this premium represents an additional compensation for the credit from an economical point of view.

Example:

The acquisition costs of the leasing object, which are the basis for calculating the leasing installments, amount to DM 60,000. The lease term is 6 years. The annual leasing installments total DM 15,000 respectively. Prior to the leasing relationship the lessee must make an one-off additional payment of DM 6,000.

In this example 6 installments are to be paid, which results in a sum of the numerical row of all installments of:

$$\frac{6}{2} \times (1 + 6) = 21$$

6. Ruling of the Federal Minister of Finance

Income tax evaluation of a real property leasing contract with degressive leasing installments

from October 10, 1983 IV B2 S. 2140 83/83

The Federal Finance Court has expressed its opinion on the income tax evaluation of a real property leasing contract with degressive leasing installments in its decision of August 12, 1982 IV R 184/79 (BStBl. II. S. 696). With reference to the results of discussions with the experts of the highest finance authorities of the individual states I make the following comments on the application of this decision:

1) Degressive Leasing Installments

In the case handled by the Federal Court of Finance, a deciding factor for the court was that the leasing agreement could only be terminated by the lessor during its total duration, and therefore during the basic leasing term, for substantial reasons, and that the amount of the annual payments to be made by the lessee during the basic leasing term were already fixed, and, in particularly, contrary to the leasing installments after the expiry of the basic lease term, could not be increased unilaterally by the lessor on the basis of market conditions. The above mentioned Federal Finance Court decision is to be applied to cases with a similar set of facts where such cases are based on real-property leasing agreements concluded after December 31, 1982. If in real-property leasing agreements concluded before January 1, 1983 the lessor and lessee have deviated from the principles of the above mentioned decision and have based their commercial and tax balance sheets on degressive leasing installments, then this may remain so.

2) Rent prepayments and special payments

The above mentioned Federal Finance court decision is to be applied in its full extent to contractually agreed rent prepayments and special payments.

1. ASSET ALLOCATED TO LESSOR

1. LESSOR

Balance Sheet		Profit and Loss Account	
ASSET	LIABILITY/ DEFERRED INCOME	DEPRECIATION INTEREST EXPENSE	LEASE PAYMENTS

2. LESSEE

Balance Sheet		Profit and Loss Account	
-	-	LEASE PAYMENTS	-

2. ASSET ALLOCATED TO LESSEE

1. LESSOR

Balance Sheet		Profit and Loss Account	
RECEIVABLE	LIABILITY	COST OF SALES INTEREST EXPENSE	SALES INTEREST INCOME

2. LESSEE

Balance Sheet		Profit and Loss Account	
ASSET	LIABILITY	DEPRECIATION INTEREST EXPENSE	-